anythink

D0710020

Little Pebble™

Mammals in the Wild
Vampire Bats
A 4D BOOK

by Kathryn Clay

PEBBLE
a capstone imprint

Download the Capstone app!

- Ask an adult to download the Capstone 4D app.
- Scan the cover and stars inside the book for additional content.

When you scan a spread, you'll find fun extra stuff to go with this book! You can also find these things on the web at www.capstone4D.com using the password: bats.00801

Pebble Books are published by Pebble
1710 Roe Crest Drive, North Mankato,
Minnesota 56003
www.mycapstone.com

Library of Congress Cataloging-in-Publication Data
Names: Clay, Kathryn, author.
Title: Vampire bats : a 4D book / by Kathryn Clay.
Description: North Mankato, Minnesota : an imprint of Pebble, [2019] | Series: Little Pebble. Mammals in the wild | Audience: Age 4-7.
Identifiers: LCCN 2018004134 (print) | LCCN 2018009141 (ebook) | ISBN 9781977100924 (eBook PDF) | ISBN 9781977100801 (hardcover) | ISBN 9781977100863 (paperback)
Subjects: LCSH: Vampire bats—Juvenile literature.
Classification: LCC QL737.C52 (ebook) | LCC QL737.C52 C53 2019 (print) | DDC 599.4/5—dc23
LC record available at https://lccn.loc.gov/2018004134

Editorial Credits
Karen Aleo, editor; Juliette Peters, designer; Tracy Cummins and Heather Mauldin, media researchers; Laura Manthe, production specialist

Photo Credits
AP Photo: Jake Schoellkopf, 21; Getty Images: Bruce Dale/National Geographic, 17, Rexford Lord, 19, ullstein bild, 7; Minden Pictures: Barry Mansell, 5; Newscom: Andrea & Chris – Fotofeeling Westend61, 11; Shutterstock: helgascandinavus, Design Element, Leonardo Mercon, 1, Michael Lynch, 9, Natalia Kuzmina, Cover, SaveJungle, 13, VectorChendol, Design Element; Thinkstock: through-my-lens, 15

Table of Contents

Up Close

The moon shines.

It is night.

Here comes a vampire bat!

Flap! Flap!

Bats have wings.

Thin skin covers the wings.

Bats are mammals.

Mammals have fur or hair.

Vampire bats are
brown or gray.

At Home

Vampire bats live in
dark places.
They live in caves and trees.

Look.

Bats live in large groups.

A group of bats is

called a colony.

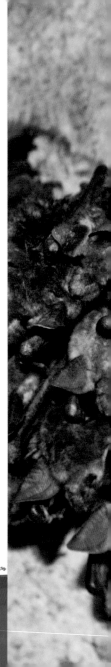

13

The bats sleep
during the day.
They eat at night.

Vampire bats drink blood.

Without blood they will die.

Bats bite pigs and cows.

Then they drink the blood.

Baby Bats

A small bat is born.

The bat drinks milk.

Soon it will drink blood.

Glossary

blood—liquid that the heart pumps through the body

cave—a large hole underground or in the side of a hill or cliff

colony—a group of bats

fur—thick hair that covers an animal

mammal—a warm-blooded animal that breathes air; mammals have hair or fur; female mammals feed milk to their young

skin—the outer covering of tissue on a body

Read More

Hirsh, Rebecca. *Vampire Bats: Nighttime Flying Mammals.* Comparing Animal Traits. Minneapolis: Lerner Publishing Group, 2015.

Jenner, Caryn. *All About Bats.* New York: DK Publishing, 2017.

Rissman, Rebecca. *Bats: Nocturnal Flyers.* Night Safari. Chicago: Heinemann Library, 2015.

Internet Sites

Use FactHound to find Internet sites related to this book.

Visit www.facthound.com

Just type in 9781977100801 and go.

Check out projects, games and lots more at
www.capstonekids.com

Critical Thinking Questions

1. What covers a bat's wings?

2. What do vampire bats drink?

3. Where do bats live?

Index